THIS BOOK
BELONGS TO

_____

_____

_____

_____

Cover and interior design by Janelle Coury

GUESTBOOK

Copyright © 2020 by Ruth Chou Simons
Published by Harvest House Publishers
Eugene, Oregon 97408
www.harvesthousepublishers.com

ISBN 978-0-7369-8092-0 (hardcover)

Library of Congress Cataloging-in-Publication Data is on file at the Library of Congress, Washington, DC.

Printed in China

HARVEST HOUSE PUBLISHERS
EUGENE, OREGON

19 20 21 22 23 24 25 26 27 28 / RDS-JC / 10 9 8 7 6 5 4 3 2 1

A home is shaped and formed by the lives of each person who walks through its doors. More than walls, rooms, and decor, a home reflects the values, joys, and wisdom of its people. Hospitality is an opportunity to both give blessing and receive it when we intentionally extend welcome. In *Foundations: 12 Biblical Truths to Shape a Family*, my husband Troy and I, grateful parents to six boys, share the values and gospel-centered truths that we long to be conformed to, starting within the walls of our home. My hope is that this *In Our Home Guestbook* serves to remind you of some of those same biblical truths—for your family's encouragement and the encouragement of those visiting your home. Take heart—you're building something beautiful day by day when you're building on the foundation of God's Word.

Because of grace,

Ruth

LOVE GOD

above all else and with all you've got.

And you shall love the Lord your God
with all your heart and with all your soul and
with all your mind and with all your strength.

MARK 12:30

name & contact   message

name & contact

message

name & contact   message

_____   _____

_____   _____

_____   _____

_____   _____

_____   _____

_____   _____

_____   _____

_____   _____

_____   _____

_____   _____

_____   _____

name & contact

message

We love because He first loved us.

1 JOHN 4:19

name & contact

message

_____

_____

_____

_____

_____

_____

_____

_____

_____

_____

_____

_____

_____

_____

_____

_____

_____

_____

_____

_____

_____

_____

name & contact   message

name & contact

message

name & contact

message

name & contact   message

name & contact

message

Teach me your way, LORD, that I may rely on your faithfulness;
give me an undivided heart, that I may fear your name.

PSALM 86:11 NIV

name & contact

message

name & contact   message

name & contact   message

BE AN
ENCOURAGER
and
BUILD EACH OTHER UP.

*Therefore encourage one another and
build one another up, just as you are doing.*

1 THESSALONIANS 5:11

name & contact   message

_____   _____
_____   _____
_____   _____
_____   _____

_____   _____
_____   _____
_____   _____

_____   _____
_____   _____
_____   _____

name & contact   message

_____   _____
_____   _____
_____   _____
_____   _____

_____   _____
_____   _____
_____   _____
_____   _____

_____   _____
_____   _____
_____   _____

name & contact   message

name & contact   message

name & contact   message

_____   _____

_____   _____

_____   _____

_____   _____

_____   _____

_____   _____

_____   _____

_____   _____

_____   _____

_____   _____

_____   _____

_____   _____

_____   _____

_____   _____

_____   _____

_____   _____

_____   _____

Speak to one another with psalms, hymns, and spiritual songs.
Sing and make music in your hearts to the Lord...

EPHESIANS 5:19 BSB

name & contact   message

_____   _____

_____   _____

_____   _____

_____   _____

_____   _____

_____   _____

_____   _____

_____   _____

_____   _____

_____   _____

_____   _____

name & contact

message

name & contact   message

name & contact

message

*Encourage one another daily, as long as it is called "Today,"
so that none of you may be hardened by sin's deceitfulness.*

HEBREWS 3:13 NIV

name & contact   message

name & contact   message

name & contact   message

name & contact   message

name & contact   *message*

give generously

IN WORD, ACTION, AND SUPPLY – THERE IS NOTHING TO LOSE.

He who supplies seed to the sower and bread for food will supply and multiply your seed for sowing and increase the harvest of your righteousness.

2 CORINTHIANS 9:10

name & contact   message

_____   _____

_____   _____

_____   _____

_____   _____

_____   _____

_____   _____

_____   _____

_____   _____

_____   _____

_____   _____

name & contact

message

_____

_____

_____

_____

_____

_____

_____

_____

Every good gift and every perfect gift is from above,
coming down from the Father of lights,
with whom there is no variation or
shadow due to change.

JAMES 1:17

name & contact

message

_____

_____

_____

_____

_____

_____

_____

_____

_____

_____

_____

_____

_____

_____

_____

_____

_____

_____

_____

_____

_____

_____

name & contact   message

name & contact   message

name & contact

message

_____
_____
_____
_____

_____
_____
_____
_____

*I tell you, do not be anxious about your life,
what you will eat or what you will drink, nor about your body,
what you will put on. Is not life more than food,
and the body more than clothing?*

MATTHEW 6:25

name & contact   message

name & contact   *message*

_____
_____
_____
_____

_____
_____
_____
_____

God loves a cheerful giver.

2 CORINTHIANS 9:7

name & contact   message

name & contact   *message*

_____   _____
_____   _____
_____   _____
_____   _____

_____   _____
_____   _____
_____   _____

Out of the abundance of the heart
his mouth speaks.

LUKE 6:45

name & contact   message

name & contact

message

name & contact   message

name & contact

message

Indeed, I count everything as loss
because of the surpassing worth of
knowing Christ Jesus my Lord.

PHILIPPIANS 3:8

name & contact   message

_____   _____
_____   _____
_____   _____
_____   _____
_____   _____
_____   _____
_____   _____
_____   _____
_____   _____
_____   _____
_____   _____

BEAR WITH
ONE ANOTHER

FORGIVE
as God has forgiven you.

Bearing with one another and,
if one has a complaint against another, forgiving each other;
as the Lord has forgiven you, so you also must forgive.

COLOSSIANS 3:13

name & contact

message

name & contact message

name & contact   message

name & contact   *message*

_____   _____

_____   _____

_____   _____

_____   _____

_____   _____

_____   _____

_____   _____

Be kind to one another, tenderhearted, forgiving one another,
as God in Christ forgave you.

EPHESIANS 4:32

name & contact   message

_____   _____

_____   _____

_____   _____

_____   _____

_____   _____

_____   _____

_____   _____

_____   _____

_____   _____

_____   _____

_____   _____

name & contact   message

name & contact   message

name & contact   message

name & contact   message

name & contact

message

By grace you have been saved through faith.
And this is not your own doing; it is the gift of God...

EPHESIANS 2:8

name & contact   message

name & contact   message

name & contact   message

name & contact   message

name & contact

message

_____
_____
_____
_____

_____
_____
_____
_____

_____
_____
_____
_____

*think of others
as God does:*
IMAGE-BEARING SOULS.

*From now on, therefore, we regard no one according to the flesh.
Even though we once regarded Christ according to the flesh,
we regard him thus no longer.*

2 CORINTHIANS 5:16

name & contact   *message*

name & contact   *message*

God created man in his own image, in the image of God he created him;
male and female he created them.

GENESIS 1:27

name & contact   message

name & contact

message

name & contact   message

_After this I looked, and there before me
was a great multitude that no one could count,
from every nation, tribe, people and language,
standing before the throne and before the Lamb._

REVELATION 7:9 NIV

name & contact

message

_____

_____

_____

_____

_____

_____

_____

_____

_____

_____

_____

_____

name & contact   message

name & contact   message

name & contact

message

_____

_____

_____

_____

_____

_____

_____

_____

_____

_____

_____

_____

_____

_____

*We are his workmanship, created in Christ Jesus for good works, which
God prepared beforehand, that we should walk in them.*

EPHESIANS 2:10

name & contact   message

name & contact   message

name & contact   message

_____   _____

_____   _____

_____   _____

_____   _____

_____   _____

_____   _____

_____   _____

_____   _____

_____   _____

_____   _____

_____   _____

KEEP YOUR HOPE in HEAVEN

and hold lightly to

THE THINGS OF EARTH.

Therefore, preparing your minds for action, and being sober-minded,
set your hope fully on the grace that will be brought to you
at the revelation of Jesus Christ.

1 PETER 1:13

name & contact   message

_____   _____

_____   _____

_____   _____

_____   _____

_____   _____

_____   _____

_____   _____

_____   _____

_____   _____

_____   _____

_____   _____

name & contact

message

Where your treasure is,
there your heart will be also.

MATTHEW 6:21

name & contact   message

_____   _____

_____   _____

_____   _____

_____   _____

_____   _____

_____   _____

_____   _____

_____   _____

_____   _____

_____   _____

_____   _____

name & contact   message

name & contact   message

name & contact   *message*

_____   _____

_____   _____

_____   _____

_____   _____

_____   _____

_____   _____

_____   _____

Now faith is the assurance of things hoped for,
the conviction of things not seen.

HEBREWS 11:1

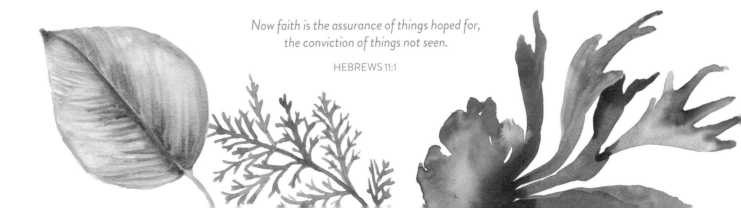

name & contact   message

name & contact   message

name & contact   message

We do not lose heart. Though our outer self is wasting away,
our inner self is being renewed day by day.

2 CORINTHIANS 4:16

name & contact   message

name & contact   message

name & contact   message

He will wipe every tear from their eyes.
There will be no more death or mourning or crying or pain,
for the old order of things has passed away.

REVELATION 21:4 NIV

Other Books available from

RUTH CHOU SIMONS